THIS JOURNAL
BELONGS TO

_____

THE DAILY QUESTION FOR YOU AND YOUR CHILD

Hardcover ISBN 978-0-525-65092-8

Published in the United States by WaterBrook, an imprint of the Crown Publishing Group, a division of Penguin Random House LLC, New York.

WaterBrook® and its deer colophon are registered trademarks of Penguin Random House LLC.

Printed in China

Book and cover design by Danielle Deschenes
Book and cover illustrations by Shutterstock © Nikolaeva

10 9 8 7 6 5 4 3 2 1

2018—First Edition

SPECIAL SALES

Most WaterBrook books are available at special quantity discounts when purchased in bulk by corporations, organizations, and special-interest groups. Custom imprinting or excerpting can also be done to fit special needs. For information, please e-mail specialmarketscms@ penguinrandomhouse.com or call 1-800-603-7051.

THE DAILY

QUESTION

FOR YOU
AND YOUR CHILD

WATERBROOK

WELCOME

— TO —

YOUR CHILD'S STORY!

KIDS GROW UP FAST! It can be hard to take the time to stop and remember all of the unique quirks and beautiful little pieces of your child's personality. With the frenetic speed of modern life, it's important to take some intentional time to bond and make lifelong memories.

The Daily Question for You and Your Child is meant to help you do just that. Every day for the next three years, this book will have a question for you to ask your child. The daily questions are all over the map. Some days you'll ask about their food and entertainment preferences, others you'll ask them to make up a short story, and other days you'll ask them about deeper issues of their heart and spirituality. Of course, this is *your* journey together, so feel free to reword, restructure, or add caveats to any of the questions you encounter. Depending on your child's age or writing ability, you might want to write as your child dictates, or they can record answers themselves. Some days, your child's responses may bring you laughter, surprise you, make you think, or even concern you. But once they've finished responding, we hope that these little moments each day or night can help lead you two into a deeper time of bonding.

This book can become a time capsule of sorts, in which you have a tangible place to watch your child grow and develop. Hopefully you'll delight in the ways you can see your child change, and some of the other ways they stay the same. But whatever journey you travel as you fill out these pages together, we hope it brings you closer as a family.

JANUARY

1

JANUARY

What is your favorite way to celebrate New Year's Eve and New Year's Day?

20___ *

20___ *

20___ *

*Did you make a New Year's resolution?
What is it?*

2
JANUARY

20___ * _____

_____

_____

_____

_____

20___ * _____

_____

_____

_____

_____

20___ * _____

_____

_____

_____

_____

3

JANUARY

What have you accomplished lately that you're proud of?

20___ *

20___ *

20___ *

Who do you think needs a hug today?

4
JANUARY

20___ *

20___ *

20___ *

5 JANUARY

If you could spend an hour as any animal, what animal would you pick?

20___ ✳ _____

_____

_____

_____

_____

20___ ✳ _____

_____

_____

_____

_____

20___ ✳ _____

_____

_____

_____

_____

What is something that you're looking forward to right now?

6
JANUARY

20___ * _____

_____

_____

_____

_____

20___ * _____

_____

_____

_____

_____

20___ * _____

_____

_____

_____

_____

7

JANUARY

Do you prefer to build snowmen or have snowball fights?

20_____ *

20_____ *

20_____ *

What is your favorite Bible story? Why?

8
JANUARY

20____ ✳ _____

_____

_____

_____

_____

20____ ✳ _____

_____

_____

_____

_____

20____ ✳ _____

_____

_____

_____

_____

9

JANUARY

What is the best thing about birthdays?

20____ *

20____ *

20____ *

What is your favorite book, and why?

10
JANUARY

20____ * _____

_____

_____

_____

_____

20____ * _____

_____

_____

_____

_____

20____ * _____

_____

_____

_____

_____

11
JANUARY

What did you do this week
that was really brave?

20____ *

_____

_____

_____

_____

_____

20____ *

_____

_____

_____

_____

_____

20____ *

_____

_____

_____

_____

_____

How could we help out the people in need in our community?

12 JANUARY

20____ *

_____

_____

_____

_____

_____

20____ *

_____

_____

_____

_____

_____

20____ *

_____

_____

_____

_____

_____

13

JANUARY

What do you like to do with your friends?

20____ *

20____ *

20____ *

How would you describe yourself?

14
JANUARY

20____ * _____
_____
_____
_____
_____

20____ * _____
_____
_____
_____
_____

20____ * _____
_____
_____
_____
_____

15
JANUARY

What was the best part of your day today?

20____ *

_____

_____

_____

_____

_____

20____ *

_____

_____

_____

_____

_____

20____ *

_____

_____

_____

_____

_____

What is the best way to show someone you're sorry?

16 JANUARY

20____ ✳ _____

_____

_____

_____

_____

20____ ✳ _____

_____

_____

_____

_____

20____ ✳ _____

_____

_____

_____

_____

17

God says you're a work of art.
How does that make you feel?

20___ ＊ _____

_____

_____

_____

_____

20___ ＊ _____

_____

_____

_____

_____

20___ ＊ _____

_____

_____

_____

_____

18 JANUARY

What did you dream about last night?

20___ * _____

_____

_____

_____

_____

20___ * _____

_____

_____

_____

_____

20___ * _____

_____

_____

_____

_____

19

JANUARY

Tell me about a time you felt misunderstood.

20____ ✳ _____

_____

_____

_____

_____

20____ ✳ _____

_____

_____

_____

_____

20____ ✳ _____

_____

_____

_____

_____

What is your least favorite chore, and why?

20

20

20

21
JANUARY

What do you think I like about going to church?

20___ *

20___ *

20___ *

How did you pick your favorite color?

22
JANUARY

20____ * _____

_____

_____

_____

_____

20____ * _____

_____

_____

_____

_____

20____ * _____

_____

_____

_____

_____

23
JANUARY

Write a short story about a puppy.

20___ *

20___ *

20___ *

If you could travel to the past, where would you go?

24
JANUARY

20___ *

20___ *

20___ *

25

JANUARY

How tall are you today?

20____ *

20____ *

20____ *

*What is your favorite thing
that we do together?*

20____ * _____

_____

_____

_____

_____

20____ * _____

_____

_____

_____

_____

20____ * _____

_____

_____

_____

_____

**26
JANUARY**

27

JANUARY

What helps you feel better when you get scared?

20____ ＊ _____

_____

_____

_____

_____

20____ ＊ _____

_____

_____

_____

_____

20____ ＊ _____

_____

_____

_____

_____

What song can you not stop singing?

28
JANUARY

20____ ✳ _____

_____

_____

_____

_____

20____ ✳ _____

_____

_____

_____

_____

20____ ✳ _____

_____

_____

_____

_____

29
JANUARY

What is inspiring to you?

20____ *

_____

_____

_____

_____

_____

20____ *

_____

_____

_____

_____

_____

20____ *

_____

_____

_____

_____

_____

*What is the best way to show
God's love to someone?*

30
JANUARY

20___ *

20___ *

20___ *

31
JANUARY

Did you like your lunch today?

20＿＿ ＊ ＿＿＿＿＿＿＿＿＿＿＿＿＿＿＿＿＿＿＿＿＿＿＿＿＿＿＿＿＿＿
＿＿＿＿＿＿＿＿＿＿＿＿＿＿＿＿＿＿＿＿＿＿＿＿＿＿＿＿＿＿＿＿＿＿＿＿
＿＿＿＿＿＿＿＿＿＿＿＿＿＿＿＿＿＿＿＿＿＿＿＿＿＿＿＿＿＿＿＿＿＿＿＿
＿＿＿＿＿＿＿＿＿＿＿＿＿＿＿＿＿＿＿＿＿＿＿＿＿＿＿＿＿＿＿＿＿＿＿＿
＿＿＿＿＿＿＿＿＿＿＿＿＿＿＿＿＿＿＿＿＿＿＿＿＿＿＿＿＿＿＿＿＿＿＿＿

20＿＿ ＊ ＿＿＿＿＿＿＿＿＿＿＿＿＿＿＿＿＿＿＿＿＿＿＿＿＿＿＿＿＿＿
＿＿＿＿＿＿＿＿＿＿＿＿＿＿＿＿＿＿＿＿＿＿＿＿＿＿＿＿＿＿＿＿＿＿＿＿
＿＿＿＿＿＿＿＿＿＿＿＿＿＿＿＿＿＿＿＿＿＿＿＿＿＿＿＿＿＿＿＿＿＿＿＿
＿＿＿＿＿＿＿＿＿＿＿＿＿＿＿＿＿＿＿＿＿＿＿＿＿＿＿＿＿＿＿＿＿＿＿＿
＿＿＿＿＿＿＿＿＿＿＿＿＿＿＿＿＿＿＿＿＿＿＿＿＿＿＿＿＿＿＿＿＿＿＿＿

20＿＿ ＊ ＿＿＿＿＿＿＿＿＿＿＿＿＿＿＿＿＿＿＿＿＿＿＿＿＿＿＿＿＿＿
＿＿＿＿＿＿＿＿＿＿＿＿＿＿＿＿＿＿＿＿＿＿＿＿＿＿＿＿＿＿＿＿＿＿＿＿
＿＿＿＿＿＿＿＿＿＿＿＿＿＿＿＿＿＿＿＿＿＿＿＿＿＿＿＿＿＿＿＿＿＿＿＿
＿＿＿＿＿＿＿＿＿＿＿＿＿＿＿＿＿＿＿＿＿＿＿＿＿＿＿＿＿＿＿＿＿＿＿＿
＿＿＿＿＿＿＿＿＿＿＿＿＿＿＿＿＿＿＿＿＿＿＿＿＿＿＿＿＿＿＿＿＿＿＿＿

FEBRUARY

1

FEBRUARY

Who is your closest friend?

20_____ *

_____

_____

_____

_____

_____

20_____ *

_____

_____

_____

_____

_____

20_____ *

_____

_____

_____

_____

_____

*What is the best present
you've ever received?*

2
FEBRUARY

20___ ✳ _____

_____

_____

_____

_____

20___ ✳ _____

_____

_____

_____

_____

20___ ✳ _____

_____

_____

_____

_____

3

FEBRUARY

Who is God?

20_____ *

_____

_____

_____

_____

_____

20_____ *

_____

_____

_____

_____

_____

20_____ *

_____

_____

_____

_____

_____

If you could build anything, what would it be?

4 FEBRUARY

20____ ✳ _____

_____

_____

_____

_____

20____ ✳ _____

_____

_____

_____

_____

20____ ✳ _____

_____

_____

_____

_____

5

FEBRUARY

What do you miss about being younger?

20___ *

20___ *

20___ *

What's exciting about growing up?

6
FEBRUARY

20___ *

_____

_____

_____

_____

20___ *

_____

_____

_____

_____

20___ *

_____

_____

_____

_____

7
FEBRUARY

What did you do this week to keep your body healthy?

20____ *

_____

_____

_____

_____

_____

20____ *

_____

_____

_____

_____

_____

20____ *

_____

_____

_____

_____

_____

What do you think heaven will be like?

8 FEBRUARY

20____ *

20____ *

20____ *

9

FEBRUARY

How have you helped our family this week?

20_____ *

20_____ *

20_____ *

Who is your hero/heroine?

10 FEBRUARY

20___ ＊ _____

_____

_____

_____

_____

20___ ＊ _____

_____

_____

_____

_____

20___ ＊ _____

_____

_____

_____

_____

11

FEBRUARY

What is your favorite holiday? Why?

20____ *

_____

_____

_____

_____

_____

20____ *

_____

_____

_____

_____

_____

20____ *

_____

_____

_____

_____

_____

12
FEBRUARY

What is something that made you laugh this week?

20____ *

_____

_____

_____

_____

20____ *

_____

_____

_____

_____

20____ *

_____

_____

_____

_____

13
FEBRUARY

*If you could ask Jesus a question,
what would you ask him?*

20___ * _____

_____

_____

_____

_____

20___ * _____

_____

_____

_____

_____

20___ * _____

_____

_____

_____

_____

How do you show love to others?

14
FEBRUARY

20___ *

_____

_____

_____

_____

20___ *

_____

_____

_____

_____

20___ *

_____

_____

_____

_____

15

FEBRUARY

What is your favorite word?

20___ * _____

_____

_____

_____

_____

20___ * _____

_____

_____

_____

_____

20___ * _____

_____

_____

_____

_____

Do you feel like you have enough free time?
Why or why not?

16
FEBRUARY

20____ * _____

_____

_____

_____

_____

20____ * _____

_____

_____

_____

_____

20____ * _____

_____

_____

_____

_____

17

FEBRUARY

*Who can you do something
nice for this week?*

20____ *

20____ *

20____ *

If you had all the money in the world, what would you buy?

18

FEBRUARY

20___ *

_____

_____

_____

_____

20___ *

_____

_____

_____

_____

20___ *

_____

_____

_____

_____

19

FEBRUARY

Name a movie you saw recently that you didn't like. Why didn't you like it?

20____ *

_____

_____

_____

_____

_____

20____ *

_____

_____

_____

_____

_____

20____ *

_____

_____

_____

_____

_____

What is your favorite song to dance to?

20___ * _____

_____

_____

_____

_____

20___ * _____

_____

_____

_____

_____

20___ * _____

_____

_____

_____

_____

21
FEBRUARY

What are three ways you'd describe our neighborhood?

20____ *

_____

_____

_____

_____

_____

20____ *

_____

_____

_____

_____

_____

20____ *

_____

_____

_____

_____

_____

What is something that I always tell you?

22

FEBRUARY

20____ * _____

_____

_____

_____

_____

20____ * _____

_____

_____

_____

_____

20____ * _____

_____

_____

_____

_____

23

FEBRUARY

*What prayer has God answered
for you lately? How do you feel about it?*

20___ * _____

_____

_____

_____

_____

20___ * _____

_____

_____

_____

_____

20___ * _____

_____

_____

_____

_____

*If I gave you a parachute,
what would you jump off?*

**24
FEBRUARY**

20____ *

20____ *

20____ *

25
FEBRUARY

Do you think robots are cool or scary? Why?

20___ *

20___ *

20___ *

What is a rule that is hard to obey?

26
FEBRUARY

20___ *

20___ *

20___ *

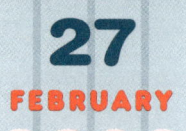

27
FEBRUARY

What makes you sad?

20___ *

_____

_____

_____

_____

_____

20___ *

_____

_____

_____

_____

_____

20___ *

_____

_____

_____

_____

_____

What is your favorite subject in school?

28
FEBRUARY

20____ *

20____ *

20____ *

MARCH

What helps you fall asleep?

1
MARCH

20____ * _____

_____

_____

_____

_____

20____ * _____

_____

_____

_____

_____

20____ * _____

_____

_____

_____

_____

2

MARCH

What brings you joy?

20___ *

20___ *

20___ *

What is your favorite worship song?

3
MARCH

20____ *

_____

_____

_____

_____

20____ *

_____

_____

_____

_____

20____ *

_____

_____

_____

_____

4

MARCH

*Did you ever want to give up on something
because you thought it was too hard?
What did you do?*

20___ * _____

_____

_____

_____

_____

20___ * _____

_____

_____

_____

_____

20___ * _____

_____

_____

_____

_____

If you could have any superpower,
what would it be?

5
MARCH

20_____ *

20_____ *

20_____ *

6

MARCH

*What is something you weren't able
to do last year that you can do this year?*

20____ ✳ _____

_____

_____

_____

_____

20____ ✳ _____

_____

_____

_____

_____

20____ ✳ _____

_____

_____

_____

_____

Who is your favorite television character? Why?

7 MARCH

20___ ✳ _____

_____

_____

_____

_____

20___ ✳ _____

_____

_____

_____

_____

20___ ✳ _____

_____

_____

_____

_____

8

MARCH

What toys have you outgrown?

20___ * _____

_____

_____

_____

_____

20___ * _____

_____

_____

_____

_____

20___ * _____

_____

_____

_____

_____

What is one of your
favorite family traditions?

9
MARCH

20___ * _____

_____

_____

_____

_____

20___ * _____

_____

_____

_____

_____

20___ * _____

_____

_____

_____

_____

10
MARCH

*Where is your favorite place
around town to visit?*

20____ ∗ _____

_____

_____

_____

_____

20____ ∗ _____

_____

_____

_____

_____

20____ ∗ _____

_____

_____

_____

_____

What is the most important thing in your life?

11 MARCH

20____ *

20____ *

20____ *

12

MARCH

Do you enjoy big storms? Why or why not?

20___ * _____

_____

_____

_____

_____

20___ * _____

_____

_____

_____

_____

20___ * _____

_____

_____

_____

_____

Would you rather go camping or go to the movies?

13
MARCH

20____ * _____

_____

_____

_____

_____

20____ * _____

_____

_____

_____

_____

20____ * _____

_____

_____

_____

_____

14

MARCH

If you could trade places with someone for a day, who would it be?

20___ *

_____

_____

_____

_____

_____

20___ *

_____

_____

_____

_____

_____

20___ *

_____

_____

_____

_____

_____

What do you like most about me?

15
MARCH

20___ ✳ ─────────────────────

─────────────────────────────

─────────────────────────────

─────────────────────────────

─────────────────────────────

20___ ✳ ─────────────────────

─────────────────────────────

─────────────────────────────

─────────────────────────────

─────────────────────────────

20___ ✳ ─────────────────────

─────────────────────────────

─────────────────────────────

─────────────────────────────

─────────────────────────────

16

MARCH

What is something that most other kids like that you don't?

20____ *

_____

_____

_____

_____

_____

20____ *

_____

_____

_____

_____

_____

20____ *

_____

_____

_____

_____

_____

Describe your best friend in three words.

17
MARCH

20_____ *

20_____ *

20_____ *

18

MARCH

When did you work your very hardest at something?

20___ *

_____

_____

_____

_____

_____

20___ *

_____

_____

_____

_____

_____

20___ *

_____

_____

_____

_____

_____

What is your favorite thing about writing in this book?

19 MARCH

20___ *

_____

_____

_____

_____

_____

20___ *

_____

_____

_____

_____

_____

20___ *

_____

_____

_____

_____

_____

20
MARCH

What do you think is the best vegetable to eat, and the worst?

20___ * _____

_____

_____

_____

_____

20___ * _____

_____

_____

_____

_____

20___ * _____

_____

_____

_____

_____

When did something turn out different than you thought it would?

21 MARCH

20___ * _____

_____

_____

_____

_____

20___ * _____

_____

_____

_____

_____

20___ * _____

_____

_____

_____

_____

22

MARCH

What do you wish I would say
to you more often?

20____ *

_____

_____

_____

_____

_____

20____ *

_____

_____

_____

_____

_____

20____ *

_____

_____

_____

_____

_____

If you could talk to a famous person, who would it be, and what would you say?

23 MARCH

20___ *

_____

_____

_____

_____

_____

20___ *

_____

_____

_____

_____

_____

20___ *

_____

_____

_____

_____

_____

24

MARCH

If you could be either a butterfly or an eagle,
which would you choose?

20_____ *

20_____ *

20_____ *

Where is the best place you have ever been?

25
MARCH

20____ ✳ _____

_____

_____

_____

_____

20____ ✳ _____

_____

_____

_____

_____

20____ ✳ _____

_____

_____

_____

_____

26
MARCH

If you could travel to any story in the Bible,
which one would you choose?

20____ *

20____ *

20____ *

If you could make up your own holiday, what would it be?

27
MARCH

20___ ✳ _____

_____

_____

_____

_____

20___ ✳ _____

_____

_____

_____

_____

20___ ✳ _____

_____

_____

_____

_____

28
MARCH

What do you like to do by yourself?

20___ * _____

_____

_____

_____

_____

20___ * _____

_____

_____

_____

_____

20___ * _____

_____

_____

_____

_____

*What is your favorite way
to celebrate Easter?*

**29
MARCH**

20___ * _____

_____

_____

_____

_____

20___ * _____

_____

_____

_____

_____

20___ * _____

_____

_____

_____

_____

30
MARCH

What makes you unique?

20___ ✳ _____

_____

_____

_____

_____

20___ ✳ _____

_____

_____

_____

_____

20___ ✳ _____

_____

_____

_____

_____

What is Easter?

31
MARCH

20___ * _____

_____

_____

_____

_____

20___ * _____

_____

_____

_____

_____

20___ * _____

_____

_____

_____

_____

APRIL

Do you like April Fools' pranks?
Why or why not?

APRIL

20___ *

_____

_____

_____

_____

_____

20___ *

_____

_____

_____

_____

_____

20___ *

_____

_____

_____

_____

_____

2
APRIL

What is your favorite thing about spring?

20____ *

_____

_____

_____

_____

_____

20____ *

_____

_____

_____

_____

_____

20____ *

_____

_____

_____

_____

_____

What makes you feel brave?

3
APRIL

20____ * _____

_____

_____

_____

_____

20____ * _____

_____

_____

_____

_____

20____ * _____

_____

_____

_____

_____

4
APRIL

*What is something that you enjoy,
even though it is really difficult?*

20____ *

_____

_____

_____

_____

_____

20____ *

_____

_____

_____

_____

_____

20____ *

_____

_____

_____

_____

_____

Describe your perfect day.

5
APRIL

20___ * _____

_____

_____

_____

_____

20___ * _____

_____

_____

_____

_____

20___ * _____

_____

_____

_____

_____

6
APRIL

What is the coolest thing you saw today?

20___ *

20___ *

20___ *

What do you want to be when you grow up?

7
APRIL

20___ *

20___ *

20___ *

8

APRIL

Do you like going to church?
Why or why not?

20___ *

20___ *

20___ *

What is your favorite color, and what does that color mean to you?

9
APRIL

20____ * _____

_____

_____

_____

_____

20____ * _____

_____

_____

_____

_____

20____ * _____

_____

_____

_____

_____

10
APRIL

What is something you'd like
to know how to make?

20____ *

20____ *

20____ *

What is a silly trick you'd like to learn?

11
APRIL

20___ * _____

_____

_____

_____

_____

20___ * _____

_____

_____

_____

_____

20___ * _____

_____

_____

_____

_____

12
APRIL

Make up a short story about a robot.

20____ * _____

_____

_____

_____

_____

20____ * _____

_____

_____

_____

_____

20____ * _____

_____

_____

_____

_____

*What is the biggest thing
you can jump over?*

**13
APRIL**

20___ *

20___ *

20___ *

14

APRIL

What do you do when you feel embarrassed?

20___ * _____

_____

_____

_____

_____

20___ * _____

_____

_____

_____

_____

20___ * _____

_____

_____

_____

_____

15
APRIL

Who around you needs encouragement? What can you do to encourage that person?

20____ * _____

_____

_____

_____

_____

20____ * _____

_____

_____

_____

_____

20____ * _____

_____

_____

_____

_____

16
APRIL

*What is your favorite thing to do
with your relatives?*

20___ *

_____
_____
_____
_____
_____

20___ *

_____
_____
_____
_____
_____

20___ *

_____
_____
_____
_____
_____

Are you afraid of the dark?
Why or why not?

17 APRIL

20___ * _____

_____

_____

_____

_____

20___ * _____

_____

_____

_____

_____

20___ * _____

_____

_____

_____

_____

18
APRIL

How do you feel when you make a mistake?

20___ *

20___ *

20___ *

What is a compliment someone has given you that made you happy?

19 APRIL

20___ *

20___ *

20___ *

20
APRIL

What is your favorite cookie?

20____ * _____

_____

_____

_____

_____

20____ * _____

_____

_____

_____

_____

20____ * _____

_____

_____

_____

_____

Who showed kindness to you recently?

21
APRIL

20_____ ✳ _____

_____

_____

_____

_____

20_____ ✳ _____

_____

_____

_____

_____

20_____ ✳ _____

_____

_____

_____

_____

22

APRIL

*What do you hope we have
for dinner next week?*

20____ *

_____

_____

_____

_____

20____ *

_____

_____

_____

_____

20____ *

_____

_____

_____

_____

What rule do you wish you could change?

23

APRIL

20____ *

_____

_____

_____

_____

20____ *

_____

_____

_____

_____

20____ *

_____

_____

_____

_____

24
APRIL

What game do you like to play?

20___ ＊ _____

_____

_____

_____

_____

20___ ＊ _____

_____

_____

_____

_____

20___ ＊ _____

_____

_____

_____

_____

Who do you wish we got to see more often?

25
APRIL

20____ ✳ _____

_____

_____

_____

_____

20____ ✳ _____

_____

_____

_____

_____

20____ ✳ _____

_____

_____

_____

_____

26

APRIL

What are three things you're grateful for?

20____ ✳ _____

_____

_____

_____

_____

20____ ✳ _____

_____

_____

_____

_____

20____ ✳ _____

_____

_____

_____

_____

What is your favorite thing God created?

27
APRIL

20____ *

20____ *

20____ *

28

APRIL

*What do you think God enjoys
most about you?*

20____ * _____

_____

_____

_____

_____

20____ * _____

_____

_____

_____

_____

20____ * _____

_____

_____

_____

_____

Do you think you'd like to have kids when you're a grown-up?

29
APRIL

20____ *

_____

_____

_____

_____

_____

20____ *

_____

_____

_____

_____

_____

20____ *

_____

_____

_____

_____

_____

30
APRIL

*What is your favorite thing
to do on a weekend?*

20____ *

_____

_____

_____

_____

_____

20____ *

_____

_____

_____

_____

_____

20____ *

_____

_____

_____

_____

_____

MAY

———— ✳ ————

1
MAY

What questions would you like to ask a teenager?

20____ *

20____ *

20____ *

2
MAY

What is your favorite memory?

20____ *

_____

_____

_____

_____

20____ *

_____

_____

_____

_____

20____ *

_____

_____

_____

_____

3

MAY

Where is heaven?

20____ *

20____ *

20____ *

Who is one person you could help this week?

4
MAY

20___ * _____

_____

_____

_____

_____

20___ * _____

_____

_____

_____

_____

20___ * _____

_____

_____

_____

_____

5

MAY

What are three things you liked about today?

20___ *

20___ *

20___ *

What is your favorite joke?

6 MAY

20 _____ *

_____

_____

_____

_____

20 _____ *

_____

_____

_____

_____

20 _____ *

_____

_____

_____

_____

7

MAY

How would you describe Jesus to someone else?

20____ *

20____ *

20____ *

Name one way you can show
Jesus's love to others.

8
MAY

20____ ✳ _____

_____

_____

_____

_____

20____ ✳ _____

_____

_____

_____

_____

20____ ✳ _____

_____

_____

_____

_____

9

MAY

*What is something kind someone
has done for you?*

20___ * _____

_____

_____

_____

_____

20___ * _____

_____

_____

_____

_____

20___ * _____

_____

_____

_____

_____

What are you worried about?

10 MAY

20___ ＊ _____

_____

_____

_____

_____

20___ ＊ _____

_____

_____

_____

_____

20___ ＊ _____

_____

_____

_____

_____

11
MAY

What do you do when you find it hard to love someone?

20 ___ *

_____

20 ___ *

_____

20 ___ *

_____

Is it easy for you to save money?

20____ *

20____ *

20____ *

13
MAY

What is your favorite instrument?

20____ *

20____ *

20____ *

If you could live next door to anyone,
who would it be?

14
MAY

20___ * _____

_____

_____

_____

_____

20___ * _____

_____

_____

_____

_____

20___ * _____

_____

_____

_____

_____

15

MAY

What do you wish you knew about me?

20____ *

_____

_____

_____

_____

_____

20____ *

_____

_____

_____

_____

_____

20____ *

_____

_____

_____

_____

_____

When do you like to pray?

20___ ✳ _____

_____

_____

_____

_____

20___ ✳ _____

_____

_____

_____

_____

20___ ✳ _____

_____

_____

_____

_____

17

MAY

If you got a surprise package in the mail,
what would you hope is in it?

20____ *

_____
_____
_____
_____
_____

20____ *

_____
_____
_____
_____
_____

20____ *

_____
_____
_____
_____
_____

What is your favorite smell?

18
MAY

20 ___ * ___

___

___

___

___

20 ___ * ___

___

___

___

___

20 ___ * ___

___

___

___

___

19
MAY

What is something new that you've learned?

20_____ *

20_____ *

20_____ *

Do you like math? Why or why not?

20___ ✳ _____

_____

_____

_____

_____

20___ ✳ _____

_____

_____

_____

_____

20___ ✳ _____

_____

_____

_____

_____

21

MAY

If you could read someone else's mind,
whose would it be?

20___ *

20___ *

20___ *

What do you hope you can do next year that you can't do now?

20____ *

_____

_____

_____

_____

_____

20____ *

_____

_____

_____

_____

20____ *

_____

_____

_____

_____

23
MAY

What new thing could you invent?

20_____ * _____

_____

_____

_____

_____

20_____ * _____

_____

_____

_____

_____

20_____ * _____

_____

_____

_____

_____

What is your favorite television show?

24

MAY

20____ *

20____ *

20____ *

25

MAY

What toys do you like to take
to bed with you?

20___ *

_____

_____

_____

_____

20___ *

_____

_____

_____

_____

20___ *

_____

_____

_____

_____

On a five-year mission to colonize Mars, you can bring two things from your room. What are they?

26
MAY

20___ * _____

_____

_____

_____

_____

20___ * _____

_____

_____

_____

_____

20___ * _____

_____

_____

_____

_____

27

MAY

Describe a sunset.

20____ ＊ _____

_____

_____

_____

_____

20____ ＊ _____

_____

_____

_____

_____

20____ ＊ _____

_____

_____

_____

_____

28
MAY

When did you have to be honest,
even though it wasn't easy?

20____ * _____

_____

_____

_____

_____

20____ * _____

_____

_____

_____

_____

20____ * _____

_____

_____

_____

_____

29
MAY

What is your favorite weather?

20___ ＊ _____

_____

_____

_____

_____

20___ ＊ _____

_____

_____

_____

_____

20___ ＊ _____

_____

_____

_____

_____

*Would you rather eat broccoli
or green beans?*

30
MAY

20___ * _____

_____

_____

_____

_____

20___ * _____

_____

_____

_____

_____

20___ * _____

_____

_____

_____

_____

31

MAY

What do you think I like most about you?

20____ *_____

_____

_____

_____

_____

20____ *_____

_____

_____

_____

_____

20____ *_____

_____

_____

_____

_____

JUNE

✳

1

JUNE

What is your favorite thing to do during the summer?

20_____ *

_____

_____

_____

_____

20_____ *

_____

_____

_____

_____

20_____ *

_____

_____

_____

_____

What do you like that most
other kids don't?

2
JUNE

20____ *

_____

_____

_____

_____

20____ *

_____

_____

_____

_____

20____ *

_____

_____

_____

_____

3

JUNE

What do you wish you could spend more time doing?

20___ *

_____

_____

_____

_____

_____

20___ *

_____

_____

_____

_____

_____

20___ *

_____

_____

_____

_____

_____

If you could have any pet, what would it be, and what would you name it?

20___ *

_____

_____

_____

_____

_____

20___ *

_____

_____

_____

_____

_____

20___ *

_____

_____

_____

_____

_____

5
JUNE

Do you think spiders are gross or cool? Why?

20 ___ ✳ _____

_____

_____

_____

_____

20 ___ ✳ _____

_____

_____

_____

_____

20 ___ ✳ _____

_____

_____

_____

_____

What is your favorite Bible verse?

6 JUNE

20___ * _____
_____
_____
_____
_____

20___ * _____
_____
_____
_____
_____

20___ * _____
_____
_____
_____
_____

7

JUNE

If you could do one thing to help kids in need around the world, what would you do?

20___ *

20___ *

20___ *

If your name wasn't your name,
what name would you pick instead?

8
JUNE

20___ *

_____

_____

_____

_____

_____

20___ *

_____

_____

_____

_____

_____

20___ *

_____

_____

_____

_____

_____

9

JUNE

What is your weirdest fear?

20___ ✳ _____

_____

_____

_____

_____

20___ ✳ _____

_____

_____

_____

_____

20___ ✳ _____

_____

_____

_____

_____

What made today different from yesterday?

10
JUNE

20___ *

20___ *

20___ *

11

JUNE

What do you do when you're bored?

20___ *

20___ *

20___ *

What is the best dream you've ever had?

12
JUNE

20____ *

20____ *

20____ *

13

JUNE

What do you like to do?

20_____ *

20_____ *

20_____ *

Who encourages you?

14
JUNE

20____ *＊* _____

_____

_____

_____

_____

20____ *＊* _____

_____

_____

_____

_____

20____ *＊* _____

_____

_____

_____

_____

15
JUNE

Where is your favorite place to go during the summer?

20___ *

20___ *

20___ *

What do you wish people knew about you?

20____ * _____

_____

_____

_____

_____

20____ * _____

_____

_____

_____

_____

20____ * _____

_____

_____

_____

_____

17

JUNE

What are five things you like that are yellow?

20_____ *

_____

_____

_____

_____

_____

20_____ *

_____

_____

_____

_____

_____

20_____ *

_____

_____

_____

_____

_____

What make-believe world in movies, books, or TV would you like to live in?

18 JUNE

20 * _____

_____

_____

_____

20 * _____

_____

_____

_____

20 * _____

_____

_____

_____

_____

19

JUNE

If you could be president for the day,
what would you do?

20____ ✳ _____

_____

_____

_____

_____

20____ ✳ _____

_____

_____

_____

_____

20____ ✳ _____

_____

_____

_____

_____

Write me a silly poem.

20____ ✳ _____

_____

_____

_____

_____

20____ ✳ _____

_____

_____

_____

_____

20____ ✳ _____

_____

_____

_____

_____

21
JUNE

Where would you hide buried treasure?

20___ * _____

_____

_____

_____

_____

20___ * _____

_____

_____

_____

_____

20___ * _____

_____

_____

_____

_____

*Write your full name
in your best penmanship.*

22
JUNE

20___ ✳ _____

_____

_____

_____

_____

20___ ✳ _____

_____

_____

_____

_____

20___ ✳ _____

_____

_____

_____

_____

23

JUNE

What do you do when you feel nervous?

20____ *

_____

_____

_____

_____

_____

20____ *

_____

_____

_____

_____

_____

20____ *

_____

_____

_____

_____

_____

What is your favorite thing about summer?

24
JUNE

20____ *

20____ *

20____ *

25

JUNE

What noises bother you?

20 ____ *

20 ____ *

20 ____ *

When do you feel the happiest?

26
JUNE

20_____ *

_____

_____

_____

_____

_____

20_____ *

_____

_____

_____

_____

_____

20_____ *

_____

_____

_____

_____

_____

27
JUNE

What is your favorite snack?

20____ ＊ _____

20____ ＊ _____

20____ ＊ _____

Why do you like your friends?

28
JUNE

20___ *

20___ *

20___ *

29

JUNE

*The Bible says God loved you
before you were born.
How does that make you feel?*

20_____ *

_____

_____

_____

_____

_____

20_____ *

_____

_____

_____

_____

_____

20_____ *

_____

_____

_____

_____

_____

*What advice would you give
to a kindergartner?*

30
JUNE

20___ * _____

_____

_____

_____

_____

20___ * _____

_____

_____

_____

_____

20___ * _____

_____

_____

_____

_____

JULY

If you could start today over, would you?

1
JULY

20___ ✳ _____

_____

_____

_____

_____

20___ ✳ _____

_____

_____

_____

_____

20___ ✳ _____

_____

_____

_____

_____

2

What would make adults more fun?

20 ___ *

20 ___ *

20 ___ *

What do you think college will be like?

3
JULY

20___ * _____

_____

_____

_____

_____

20___ * _____

_____

_____

_____

_____

20___ * _____

_____

_____

_____

_____

4
JULY

How do you like to celebrate
the Fourth of July?

20____ *

_____

_____

_____

_____

_____

20____ *

_____

_____

_____

_____

_____

20____ *

_____

_____

_____

_____

_____

Have you ever stayed to help someone instead of leaving to play? How did it make you feel?

5
JULY

20_____ *

_____

_____

_____

_____

_____

20_____ *

_____

_____

_____

_____

_____

20_____ *

_____

_____

_____

_____

_____

6
JULY

If you could either be an international rock star or discover the cure to cancer, which would you choose?

20____ ✳ _____

_____

_____

_____

_____

20____ ✳ _____

_____

_____

_____

_____

20____ ✳ _____

_____

_____

_____

_____

If you could be a superhero,
which one would you be?

7
JULY

20___ ✳ _____

_____

_____

_____

_____

20___ ✳ _____

_____

_____

_____

_____

20___ ✳ _____

_____

_____

_____

_____

8

JULY

Who is in heaven?

20____ *

_____

_____

_____

_____

_____

20____ *

_____

_____

_____

_____

_____

20____ *

_____

_____

_____

_____

Who do you look up to?

9
JULY

20___ * _____

_____

_____

_____

_____

20___ * _____

_____

_____

_____

_____

20___ * _____

_____

_____

_____

_____

10
JULY

What do you need to change your attitude about today?

20____ ✳ _____

_____

_____

_____

_____

20____ ✳ _____

_____

_____

_____

_____

20____ ✳ _____

_____

_____

_____

_____

*What is something funny
that happened to you?*

11
JULY

20___ ✳ _____

_____

_____

_____

20___ ✳ _____

_____

_____

_____

20___ ✳ _____

_____

_____

_____

12
JULY

What do you know about Jesus?

20____ *

20____ *

20____ *

What is on your mind, no matter how small, that you want to tell Jesus?

13
JULY

20___ * _____

_____

_____

_____

_____

20___ * _____

_____

_____

_____

_____

20___ * _____

_____

_____

_____

_____

14
JULY

Are you saving up to buy something?
What is it?

20____ * _____

_____

_____

_____

_____

20____ * _____

_____

_____

_____

_____

20____ * _____

_____

_____

_____

_____

What is your favorite song?

15
JULY

20_____ *

20_____ *

20_____ *

16

JULY

What is one of the best things about our neighborhood?

20___ *

20___ *

20___ *

What do you wish I did more of?

17
JULY

20____ *

20____ *

20____ *

18
JULY

How can you make someone laugh today?

20 ____ *

_____

_____

_____

_____

_____

20 ____ *

_____

_____

_____

_____

_____

20 ____ *

_____

_____

_____

_____

_____

What do you like to pretend?

19
JULY

20_____ * _____

_____

_____

_____

_____

20_____ * _____

_____

_____

_____

_____

20_____ * _____

_____

_____

_____

_____

20
JULY

Who can you pray for tonight?

20____ *

20____ *

20____ *

What are your favorite toys?

21
JULY

20___ ✳ _____

_____

_____

_____

_____

20___ ✳ _____

_____

_____

_____

_____

20___ ✳ _____

_____

_____

_____

_____

22

JULY

What would you change about school?

20___ ✱ _____

_____

_____

_____

_____

20___ ✱ _____

_____

_____

_____

_____

20___ ✱ _____

_____

_____

_____

_____

Do you like writing? Why or why not?

23
JULY

20____ ✳ _____

20____ ✳ _____

20____ ✳ _____

24

JULY

What other language would you like to learn someday?

20___ *

20___ *

20___ *

What do you think "grace" means?

25
JULY

20___ *

_____

_____

_____

_____

20___ *

_____

_____

_____

_____

20___ *

_____

_____

_____

_____

26

What is something you're really good at?

20 _____ * _____

_____

_____

_____

_____

20 _____ * _____

_____

_____

_____

_____

20 _____ * _____

_____

_____

_____

_____

What is your favorite cartoon? Why?

27
JULY

20___ *

20___ *

20___ *

28

If you could pick a new family tradition,
what would you like it to be?

20＿＿ ＊ ＿＿＿＿＿＿＿＿＿＿＿＿＿＿＿＿＿＿＿＿＿＿

＿＿＿＿＿＿＿＿＿＿＿＿＿＿＿＿＿＿＿＿＿＿＿＿＿＿＿＿

＿＿＿＿＿＿＿＿＿＿＿＿＿＿＿＿＿＿＿＿＿＿＿＿＿＿＿＿

＿＿＿＿＿＿＿＿＿＿＿＿＿＿＿＿＿＿＿＿＿＿＿＿＿＿＿＿

＿＿＿＿＿＿＿＿＿＿＿＿＿＿＿＿＿＿＿＿＿＿＿＿＿＿＿＿

20＿＿ ＊ ＿＿＿＿＿＿＿＿＿＿＿＿＿＿＿＿＿＿＿＿＿＿

＿＿＿＿＿＿＿＿＿＿＿＿＿＿＿＿＿＿＿＿＿＿＿＿＿＿＿＿

＿＿＿＿＿＿＿＿＿＿＿＿＿＿＿＿＿＿＿＿＿＿＿＿＿＿＿＿

＿＿＿＿＿＿＿＿＿＿＿＿＿＿＿＿＿＿＿＿＿＿＿＿＿＿＿＿

＿＿＿＿＿＿＿＿＿＿＿＿＿＿＿＿＿＿＿＿＿＿＿＿＿＿＿＿

20＿＿ ＊ ＿＿＿＿＿＿＿＿＿＿＿＿＿＿＿＿＿＿＿＿＿＿

＿＿＿＿＿＿＿＿＿＿＿＿＿＿＿＿＿＿＿＿＿＿＿＿＿＿＿＿

＿＿＿＿＿＿＿＿＿＿＿＿＿＿＿＿＿＿＿＿＿＿＿＿＿＿＿＿

＿＿＿＿＿＿＿＿＿＿＿＿＿＿＿＿＿＿＿＿＿＿＿＿＿＿＿＿

＿＿＿＿＿＿＿＿＿＿＿＿＿＿＿＿＿＿＿＿＿＿＿＿＿＿＿＿

What one place do you want to visit above all others?

29
JULY

20___ * _____

_____

_____

_____

_____

20___ * _____

_____

_____

_____

_____

20___ * _____

_____

_____

_____

_____

30

JULY

What do you like to do on long car rides?

20___ *

_____

20___ *

_____

20___ *

_____

Do you prefer sunrises or sunsets? Why?

31
JULY

20_____ ✳ _____

_____

_____

_____

_____

20_____ ✳ _____

_____

_____

_____

_____

20_____ ✳ _____

_____

_____

_____

_____

AUGUST

When did you last have to be brave?

1
AUGUST

20___ *

20___ *

20___ *

2

AUGUST

What do you like to do when it rains?

20＿＿ *

20＿＿ *

20＿＿ *

Would you rather spend the day with Superman or Spider-Man?

3
AUGUST

20___ * _____
_____
_____
_____
_____

20___ * _____
_____
_____
_____
_____

20___ * _____
_____
_____
_____
_____

4

AUGUST

*What do you wish you could
spend less time doing?*

20 ___ *

20 ___ *

20 ___ *

What is your favorite animal, and why?

5
AUGUST

20___ *

20___ *

20___ *

6

AUGUST

If you could meet someone from the Bible, who would it be?

20___ *

_____
_____
_____
_____
_____

20___ *

_____
_____
_____
_____
_____

20___ *

_____
_____
_____
_____
_____

What didn't you like about today,
and how could it have been better?

7
AUGUST

20___ *

20___ *

20___ *

8
AUGUST

What is one thing you wish you could get rid of forever?

20___ ＊ _____

_____

_____

_____

_____

20___ ＊ _____

_____

_____

_____

_____

20___ ＊ _____

_____

_____

_____

_____

*What is your favorite thing
to do outside?*

**9
AUGUST**

20___ *

20___ *

20___ *

10
AUGUST

If you could solve any problem,
what would it be?

20_____ *

_____

20_____ *

_____

20_____ *

_____

*What is something you want
to accomplish tomorrow?*

**11
AUGUST**

20_____ ∗ _____

20_____ ∗ _____

20_____ ∗ _____

12

*How did you show kindness
to someone today?*

20____ *

20____ *

20____ *

*What time of day do you
most look forward to? Why?*

13
AUGUST

20___ * _____

_____

_____

_____

_____

20___ * _____

_____

_____

_____

_____

20___ * _____

_____

_____

_____

_____

14
AUGUST

What is your favorite shirt, and why do you like it?

20___ * ___

20___ *

20___ *

Have you ever gotten lost?
What did you do?

15
AUGUST

20____ ✳ _____

_____

_____

_____

_____

20____ ✳ _____

_____

_____

_____

_____

20____ ✳ _____

_____

_____

_____

_____

16
AUGUST

What is the craziest thing you've ever done?

20____ *

20____ *

20____ *

Tell me about the last time
you were sick.

17
AUGUST

20____ * _____

_____

_____

_____

_____

20____ * _____

_____

_____

_____

_____

20____ * _____

_____

_____

_____

_____

18

AUGUST

*Do you feel safer when you're alone
or with people? Why?*

20_____ *

20_____ *

20_____ *

What are five things you like that are blue?

19
AUGUST

20___ *

20___ *

20___ *

20

AUGUST

What talent do you wish you had?

20____ *

20____ *

20____ *

*Make up a short story about
a talking grapefruit.*

21
AUGUST

20____ *

20____ *

20____ *

22
AUGUST

*What imaginary creature
do you wish was real?*

20___ *

20___ *

20___ *

What do you do if you have a nightmare?

23
AUGUST

20___ *

_____

_____

_____

_____

_____

20___ *

_____

_____

_____

_____

_____

20___ *

_____

_____

_____

_____

_____

24
AUGUST

How do you feel today?

20___ *

20___ *

20___ *

What do you do when you want to calm down and feel peaceful?

25

AUGUST

20___ *

20___ *

20___ *

26

*What would you like to learn
to cook by yourself?*

20___ *

_____

_____

_____

_____

_____

20___ *

_____

_____

_____

_____

_____

20___ *

_____

_____

_____

_____

_____

Name someone who makes you smile, and explain why.

27
AUGUST

20____ * _____

_____

_____

_____

_____

20____ * _____

_____

_____

_____

_____

20____ * _____

_____

_____

_____

_____

28

AUGUST

What is your favorite food?

20___ *

20___ *

20___ *

Do you know someone who needs a friend?

29
AUGUST

20___ *

20___ *

20___ *

30

*What do you do when you disagree
with your friends?*

20___ *

20___ *

20___ *

Name three special qualities
God designed in you.

31
AUGUST

20___ *

20___ *

20___ *

SEPTEMBER

What do you love to do in the fall?

1
SEPTEMBER

20___ ✳ _____

_____

_____

_____

_____

20___ ✳ _____

_____

_____

_____ _____

_____

20___ ✳ _____

_____

_____

_____

_____

2

SEPTEMBER

*What is your favorite thing
in God's creation?*

20 ____ *

20 ____ *

20 ____ *

Who do you want to be like
when you grow up?

3
SEPTEMBER

20___ * _____

_____

_____

_____

_____

20___ * _____

_____

_____

_____

_____

20___ * _____

_____

_____

_____

_____

4

SEPTEMBER

How do you want to be remembered?

20_____ *

_____

_____

_____

_____

_____

20_____ *

_____

_____

_____

_____

_____

20_____ *

_____

_____

_____

_____

What is the first memory you can think of?

5
SEPTEMBER

20____ *

20____ *

20____ *

6

SEPTEMBER

What is something that happened in the last school year that you hope you'll remember forever?

20___ * _____

_____

_____

_____

_____

20___ * _____

_____

_____

_____

_____

20___ * _____

_____

_____

_____

_____

Who do you miss?

7
SEPTEMBER

20___ ✳ _____

_____

_____

_____

_____

20___ ✳ _____

_____

_____

_____

_____

20___ ✳ _____

_____

_____

_____

_____

8

SEPTEMBER

Who is brave?

20___ *

20___ *

20___ *

What was the most interesting thing
you saw or experienced today?

9
SEPTEMBER

20____ *

_____

_____

_____

_____

20____ *

_____

_____

_____

_____

20____ *

_____

_____

_____

_____

10
SEPTEMBER

Who makes you laugh the most?

20____ *

20____ *

20____ *

When do you feel Jesus's love the most?

11
SEPTEMBER

20 _____ *

20 _____ *

20 _____ *

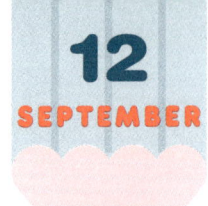

12

SEPTEMBER

What is your favorite movie?

20____ * ______________________________

20____ * ______________________________

20____ * ______________________________

What song do you like to sing?

13
SEPTEMBER

20___ *

20___ *

20___ *

14

*What do you wish I would
understand about you?*

20___ ⁕ _____

_____

_____

_____

_____

20___ ⁕ _____

_____

_____

_____

_____

20___ ⁕ _____

_____

_____

_____

_____

Who do you think could use our prayers?

15
SEPTEMBER

20___ *

_____

_____

_____

_____

20___ *

_____

_____

_____

_____

20___ *

_____

_____

_____

_____

16

SEPTEMBER

What is your favorite thing in fall?

20___ *

20___ *

20___ *

Tell me one thing you learned today.

17

SEPTEMBER

20___ *

20___ *

20___ *

18

SEPTEMBER

Who is your favorite teacher?

20___ * _____

_____

_____

_____

_____

20___ * _____

_____

_____

_____

_____

20___ * _____

_____

_____

_____

_____

What is something you find easy?

19
SEPTEMBER

20____ *

_____

_____

_____

_____

20____ *

_____

_____

_____

_____

20____ *

_____

_____

_____

_____

20
SEPTEMBER

What is something you could teach someone else?

20____ * _____

_____

_____

_____

_____

20____ * _____

_____

_____

_____

_____

20____ * _____

_____

_____

_____

_____

If you could live anywhere in the world, where would you live?

21

SEPTEMBER

20___ ✳ _____

_____

_____

_____

_____

20___ ✳ _____

_____

_____

_____

_____

20___ ✳ _____

_____

_____

_____

_____

22

SEPTEMBER

Did you try something new today?

20____ *

20____ *

20____ *

Have you ever been on an airplane?
Did you like it?

23
SEPTEMBER

20___ *

20___ *

20___ *

24

SEPTEMBER

Would you rather it be snowy or sunny?

20____ *

_____

_____

_____

_____

_____

20____ *

_____

_____

_____

_____

_____

20____ *

_____

_____

_____

_____

_____

If you had a pet dinosaur,
what name would you give it?

25
SEPTEMBER

20___ * _____

_____

_____

_____

_____

20___ * _____

_____

_____

_____

_____

20___ * _____

_____

_____

_____

_____

26
SEPTEMBER

*What person or animal in the Bible
would you like to be for one day, and why?*

20___ *

20___ *

20___ *

What is one thing you couldn't live without?

27
SEPTEMBER

20____ ＊ _____

_____

_____

_____

_____

20____ ＊ _____

_____

_____

_____

_____

20____ ＊ _____

_____

_____

_____

_____

28

SEPTEMBER

*What is the first thing you like
to do in the morning?*

20____ *

20____ *

20____ *

What is hard for you right now?
How can I help you with it?

29
SEPTEMBER

20___ *

_____

_____

_____

_____

20___ *

_____

_____

_____

_____

20___ *

_____

_____

_____

_____

30
SEPTEMBER

What do you not like to do?

20___ *

_____

20___ *

_____

20___ *

_____

OCTOBER

1

OCTOBER

*Do you prefer the house
to be noisy or quiet?*

20___ *

20___ *

20___ *

When you feel tired, do you like to be alone or with your friends?

2
OCTOBER

20___ *

20___ *

20___ *

3

OCTOBER

*If you could do something crazy
with your hair, what would you do?*

20____ *

20____ *

20____ *

Do you think you are competitive? Why?

4
OCTOBER

20___ * _____

_____

_____

_____

_____

20___ * _____

_____

_____

_____

_____

20___ * _____

_____

_____

_____

_____

5
OCTOBER

What's something you know that makes you feel smart?

20___ * _____

_____

_____

_____

_____

20___ * _____

_____

_____

_____

_____

20___ * _____

_____

_____

_____

_____

What are you really good at?

6
OCTOBER

20___ * _____

_____

_____

_____

_____

20___ * _____

_____

_____

_____

_____

20___ * _____

_____

_____

_____

_____

7

OCTOBER

If you had a cardboard box,
what would you do with it?

20_____ *

_____

20_____ *

_____

20_____ *

_____

Make up a short story
about going into space.

8
OCTOBER

20_____ *

20_____ *

20_____ *

9

OCTOBER

Are you afraid of bugs,
or do you think they're cool?

20____ *

20____ *

20____ *

What character from a book, movie, or TV show are you happy isn't real?

10
OCTOBER

20____ *

_____

_____

_____

_____

_____

20____ *

_____

_____

_____

_____

_____

20____ *

_____

_____

_____

_____

_____

11

OCTOBER

What makes you happy?

20___ *

_____

_____

_____

_____

_____

20___ *

_____

_____

_____

_____

_____

20___ *

_____

_____

_____

_____

_____

If you could only eat one food all week, what would you pick?

12 OCTOBER

20____ * _____

_____

_____

_____

_____

20____ * _____

_____

_____

_____

_____

20____ * _____

_____

_____

_____

_____

13

OCTOBER

What quality do you like best in a friend?

20___ *

20___ *

20___ *

What makes you a good friend?

14
OCTOBER

20___ ✳ _____

_____

_____

_____

_____

20___ ✳ _____

_____

_____

_____

_____

20___ ✳ _____

_____

_____

_____

_____

15

OCTOBER

What are your three favorite things about God?

20____ *

20____ *

20____ *

What do you like about today's weather?

16
OCTOBER

20____ *

_____

_____

_____

_____

_____

20____ *

_____

_____

_____

_____

_____

20____ *

_____

_____

_____

_____

_____

17

OCTOBER

*What do you hope you never forget
when you grow up?*

20____ * _____

_____

_____

_____

_____

20____ * _____

_____

_____

_____

_____

20____ * _____

_____

_____

_____

_____

What age feels really old to you?

18
OCTOBER

20____ * _____

_____

_____

_____

_____

20____ * _____

_____

_____

_____

_____

20____ * _____

_____

_____

_____

_____

19

OCTOBER

What made you laugh today?

20_____ *

20_____ *

20_____ *

What do you need most from Jesus today?

20
OCTOBER

20___ * _____

_____

_____

_____

_____

20___ * _____

_____

_____

_____

_____

20___ * _____

_____

_____

_____

_____

21

OCTOBER

What do you think I do while you're at school?

20___ * _____

_____

_____

_____

_____

20___ * _____

_____

_____

_____

_____

20___ * _____

_____

_____

_____

_____

What prayer are you still waiting on an answer for? Is it hard to wait for an answer?

22 OCTOBER

20 ___ *

_____

_____

_____

_____

_____

20 ___ *

_____

_____

_____

_____

_____

20 ___ *

_____

_____

_____

_____

_____

23

OCTOBER

What is your favorite subject in school?

20___ *

20___ *

20___ *

If you could change one thing from today,
what would it be?

24
OCTOBER

20___ * _____

_____
_____
_____
_____

20___ * _____

_____
_____
_____
_____

20___ * _____

_____
_____
_____
_____

25
OCTOBER

Where is your favorite place to be?

20____ *

20____ *

20____ *

If you could travel far into space or deep into the ocean, which would you choose and why?

26
OCTOBER

20___ *

20___ *

20___ *

27

Would you rather have the ability to fly or have a pet dinosaur?

20_____ *

_____

_____

_____

_____

_____

20_____ *

_____

_____

_____

_____

20_____ *

_____

_____

_____

_____

What is your favorite kind of bug?

28
OCTOBER

20___ *

20___ *

20___ *

29

OCTOBER

If you could be friends with any person in the Bible (other than Jesus), who would it be?

20___ *

20___ *

20___ *

*What sport or game do you
like to play the most?*

30
OCTOBER

20____ ✳ _____

_____

_____

_____

_____

20____ ✳ _____

_____

_____

_____

_____

20____ ✳ _____

_____

_____

_____

_____

31

OCTOBER

What is scary to you?

20___ *

20___ *

20___ *

NOVEMBER

——— ✳ ———

1

NOVEMBER

Name three people you are thankful for, and why you're thankful for them.

20____ *

20____ *

20____ *

What is something that confuses you?

2
NOVEMBER

20____ * _____

_____

_____

_____

_____

20____ * _____

_____

_____

_____

_____

20____ * _____

_____

_____

_____

_____

3

NOVEMBER

When was the last time you wanted to quit something? Did you?

20___ * _____

_____

_____

_____

_____

20___ * _____

_____

_____

_____

_____

20___ * _____

_____

_____

_____

_____

What is the first thing or person you think about when you wake up?

4
NOVEMBER

20____ *

20____ *

20____ *

5
NOVEMBER

Do you like to stay up late or get up early?

20_____ *

20_____ *

20_____ *

What is the coolest trick you can do?

6
NOVEMBER

20____ ✳ _____

_____

_____

_____

_____

20____ ✳ _____

_____

_____

_____

_____

20____ ✳ _____

_____

_____

_____

_____

7

NOVEMBER

*Write a short story about
going back in time.*

20____ *

20____ *

20____ *

What are three possessions that you are thankful for? Why?

8
NOVEMBER

20___ ✳ _____

_____

_____

_____

_____

20___ ✳ _____

_____

_____

_____

_____

20___ ✳ _____

_____

_____

_____

_____

9

NOVEMBER

Make up a monster you would
like and then describe it.

20___ *

20___ *

20___ *

If you were a pirate, what would be in your treasure chest?

10
NOVEMBER

20___ * _____

_____

_____

_____

_____

20___ * _____

_____

_____

_____

_____

20___ * _____

_____

_____

_____

_____

11

NOVEMBER

Are you afraid of heights?

20____ *

20____ *

20____ *

12
NOVEMBER

What would happen if you thanked God
for at least three things every day?
If you don't know, why don't you try it out?

20_____ *

_____

_____

_____

_____

_____

20_____ *

_____

_____

_____

_____

_____

20_____ *

_____

_____

_____

_____

_____

13
NOVEMBER

What makes you feel embarrassed?

20___ *

20___ *

20___ *

What are you worried about?

14

NOVEMBER

20___ *

20___ *

20___ *

15
NOVEMBER

What is your favorite ice cream?

20 ___ *

20 ___ *

20 ___ *

What makes you feel angry?

16
NOVEMBER

20___ * _____

_____

_____

_____

_____

20___ * _____

_____

_____

_____

_____

20___ * _____

_____

_____

_____

_____

17
NOVEMBER

What do you think would happen if you ate a whole pizza?

20____ *

20____ *

20____ *

How do you feel when someone forgives you?

18
NOVEMBER

20___ *

20___ *

20___ *

19
NOVEMBER

Who do you love playing with?

20___ * _____
_____
_____
_____
_____

20___ * _____
_____
_____
_____
_____

20___ * _____
_____
_____
_____
_____

What is Thanksgiving about?

20____ *

20____ *

20____ *

21

NOVEMBER

What is your favorite game to play with your friends?

20____ *

20____ *

20____ *

*Where is your favorite place
to celebrate Thanksgiving?*

22
NOVEMBER

20____ ✱ _____

_____

_____

_____

_____

20____ ✱ _____

_____

_____

_____

_____

20____ ✱ _____

_____

_____

_____

_____

23
NOVEMBER

God says he knows you inside and out,
every bone in your body.
How does that make you feel?

20_____ * _____

_____

_____

_____

_____

20_____ * _____

_____

_____

_____

_____

20_____ * _____

_____

_____

_____

_____

What is one way you can serve those around you today?

24 NOVEMBER

20___ *

_____

_____

_____

_____

_____

20___ *

_____

_____

_____

_____

_____

20___ *

_____

_____

_____

_____

_____

25
NOVEMBER

What song about God do you like to sing, and why?

20____ *

_____

20____ *

_____

20____ *

_____

What problem do you hope is fixed by the time you're my age?

26
NOVEMBER

20___ * _____

_____

_____

_____

_____

20___ * _____

_____

_____

_____

_____

20___ * _____

_____

_____

_____

_____

27

What do you think will be the best part about being an adult one day?

20____ *

_____ _____

_____

_____

_____

_____

20____ *

_____

_____

_____

_____

20____ *

_____

_____

_____

_____

_____

*Make up your own special question
and then answer it.*

28

NOVEMBER

20___ * _____

_____

_____

_____

_____

20___ * _____

_____

_____

_____

_____

20___ * _____

_____

_____

_____

_____

29
NOVEMBER

What can you do today that would make someone smile?

20___ *

20___ *

20___ *

What do I do that you think is weird?

30
NOVEMBER

20____ * _____

_____

_____

_____

_____

20____ * _____

_____

_____

_____

_____

20____ * _____

_____

_____

_____

_____

DECEMBER

What do you like about Christmas?

1
DECEMBER

20____ ✳ _____

_____

_____

_____

_____

20____ ✳ _____

_____

_____

_____

_____

20____ ✳ _____

_____

_____

_____

_____

2
DECEMBER

*What is the best and worst
thing about school?*

20 ___ *

20 ___ *

20 ___ *

What do you like to do at recess or at the park?

3
DECEMBER

20____ *

20____ *

20____ *

4

DECEMBER

*What's the best thing that happened
so far this year?*

20____ *

20____ *

20____ *

In the Christmas story, which person or animal would you have liked to be, and why?

5 DECEMBER

20___ * _____

_____

_____

_____

_____

20___ * _____

_____

_____

_____

_____

20___ * _____

_____

_____

_____

_____

6

DECEMBER

*If you could go anywhere in the world,
where would you go, and why?*

20___ *

_____

_____

_____

_____

_____

20___ *

_____

_____

_____

_____

_____

20___ *

_____

_____

_____

_____

_____

*Would you rather play sports
or draw a picture?*

7
DECEMBER

20____ * _____

_____

_____

_____

_____

20____ * _____

_____

_____

_____

_____

20____ * _____

_____

_____

_____

_____

8

DECEMBER

Do thunderstorms scare you?

20___ * ___

20___ * ___

20___ * ___

9

DECEMBER

*What gift would you have given
the Baby Jesus? How can you give
Jesus a gift now?*

20____ * _____

_____

_____

_____

_____

20____ * _____

_____

_____

_____

_____

20____ * _____

_____

_____

_____

_____

10

If you could visit a planet in our solar system, which one would it be?

20____ *

20____ *

20____ *

What is Christmas?

11
DECEMBER

20____ *

_____

_____

_____

_____

_____

20____ *

_____

_____

_____

_____

_____

20____ *

_____

_____

_____

_____

_____

12
DECEMBER

*Do you think a dragon
would make a good pet?*

20 ___ *

20 ___ *

20 ___ *

*What is the last thing you think
about before you fall asleep?*

13
DECEMBER

20____ * _____

_____

_____

_____

_____

20____ * _____

_____

_____

_____

_____

20____ * _____

_____

_____

_____

_____

14
DECEMBER

What do you want for Christmas?

20___ *

_____

20___ *

_____

20___ *

_____

Is there something you can't stop thinking about? What is it?

15 DECEMBER

20___ * _____

_____

_____

_____

_____

20___ * _____

_____

_____

_____

_____

20___ * _____

_____

_____

_____

_____

16
DECEMBER

What is your favorite junk food?

20____ *

_____

_____

_____

_____

_____

20____ *

_____

_____

_____

_____

_____

20____ *

_____

_____

_____

_____

_____

What does your best friend do to make you happy?

17
DECEMBER

20____ * _____

_____

_____

_____

_____

20____ * _____

_____

_____

_____

_____

20____ * _____

_____

_____

_____

_____

18
DECEMBER

What is your favorite Christmas song?

20___ ＊ _____

_____

_____

_____

_____

20___ ＊ _____

_____

_____

_____

_____

20___ ＊ _____

_____

_____

_____

_____

What do you wish your friends knew about you?

19
DECEMBER

20___ *

_____

_____

_____

_____

_____

20___ *

_____

_____

_____

_____

_____

20___ *

_____

_____

_____

_____

_____

20

DECEMBER

How does God communicate with you?

20___ * _____

_____

_____

_____

_____

20___ * _____

_____

_____

_____

_____

20___ * _____

_____

_____

_____

_____

*If you could give a present to someone,
who would it be?*

20___ *

_____

_____

_____

_____

_____

20___ *

_____

_____

_____

_____

_____

20___ *

_____

_____

_____

_____

_____

22
DECEMBER

*If you could ask God any question,
what would it be?*

20____ * _____

_____

_____

_____

_____

20____ * _____

_____

_____

_____

_____

20____ * _____

_____

_____

_____

_____

What is your favorite Christmas movie?

23
DECEMBER

20___ * _____

_____

_____

_____

_____

20___ * _____

_____

_____

_____

_____

20___ * _____

_____

_____

_____

_____

24

DECEMBER

How do you think your life will be different in five or ten years?

20___ ＊ _____

_____

_____

_____

_____

20___ ＊ _____

_____

_____

_____

_____

20___ ＊ _____

_____

_____

_____

_____

25

DECEMBER

Where is your favorite place
to celebrate Christmas?

20___ *

_____
_____
_____
_____
_____

20___ *

_____
_____
_____
_____
_____

20___ *

_____
_____
_____
_____
_____

26

DECEMBER

What do you want to be like when you grow up?

20____ *

20____ *

20____ *

If Jesus hung out with you today in the flesh, what would you like to do with him? Why?

27
DECEMBER

20___ * _____

_____

_____

_____

_____

20___ * _____

_____

_____

_____

_____

20___ * _____

_____

_____

_____

_____

28
DECEMBER

How do you feel about sitting in school all day?

20___ ✳ _____

_____

_____

_____

_____

20___ ✳ _____

_____

_____

_____

_____

20___ ✳ _____

_____

_____

_____

_____

What would be the best vacation you could ever go on?

29
DECEMBER

20____ *

20____ *

20____ *

30
DECEMBER

What do you love to do in the winter?

20___ *

_____

_____

_____

_____

_____

20___ *

_____

_____

_____

_____

_____

20___ *

_____

_____

_____

_____

What is something you'd like to accomplish next year?

31
DECEMBER

20___ *

_____

_____

_____

_____

20___ *

_____

_____

_____

_____

20___ *

_____

_____

_____

_____

ACKNOWLEDGMENTS

The Daily Question for You and Your Child development team is grateful to all the individuals and departments within the Crown Division and WaterBrook for their help in creating this project.

A special thank you goes to the following people who contributed questions for the book:

Laura Barker
Christina Brandsma
Leslie Calhoun
Kendall Davis
Jessica Lamb
Kristopher Orr
Bruce Nygren
Jennifer Reyes
Pam Shoup
Susan Tjaden
Kim Von Fange
Ericka Weed
Laura Wright

DEVELOPMENT TEAM
Kendall Davis
Douglass Mann
Susan Tjaden